Living in a Castle

R J UNSTEAD

Illustrated by
Victor Ambrus

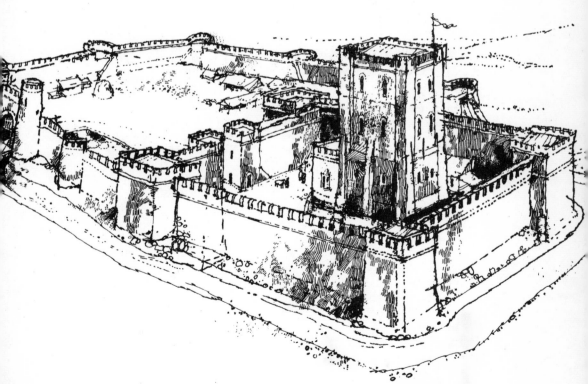

A & C Black · London

The 'Living in' series

Living in a Castle	ISBN 0 7136 1088 3
Living in a Crusader Land	ISBN 0 7136 1081 6
Living in a Medieval City	ISBN 0 7136 1090 5
Living in a Medieval Village	ISBN 0 7136 1089 1

A & C Black Ltd
4 Soho Square
London WIV 6AD

ISBN 0 7136 1088 3

© 1971 A & C Black Ltd

Printed and bound in Great Britain by
Bookprint International Limited.

Contents

Wenworth Castle

Living in a castle

By the middle of the thirteenth century, there were at least 300 castles in England. A traveller would seldom ride all day without seeing one of these great fortresses. Its whitewashed towers and walls dominated the countryside, dwarfing the villages with their thatched huts and timber manor-houses.

Some of the castles belonged to the king, but most were held by the great barons of the realm. A castle was the proof of a baron's power and rank. It had to be big enough to house his followers and strong enough to protect his lands from enemies. If he was very rich, he probably had several castles in different parts of the country, each standing in a great estate whose manors supplied men, money and food for the baronial household.

Men-at-arms

The baron had to keep the castle defences in good order and up to date with the latest ideas of warfare. He well knew that some of his fellow barons were always ready to pick a quarrel and to make a sudden attack upon a neighbour. At times, they defied the authority of the king himself.

So, every great lord kept a company of knights and men-at-arms who served him for pay, and for land which he might grant them. In time of need, his tenants, i.e. those who held land of him, had to do *castle-guard* which meant coming to the castle to man its defences.

Yet the castle was also the baron's home where he and his family lived, worked and enjoyed themselves. Many servants and officials were needed in these great households which sometimes numbered a hundred or more persons.

Let us see what life was like in a castle in about the year 1250.

Portcullis and drawbridge

Wenworth Castle

Wenworth Castle stood, let us say, somewhere in southern England. Its lord, the Earl Richard, possessed two other castles, one in the Midlands and one in Norfolk, and every few months he moved from one to another. In this way, he saw that his estates were properly run and his household could eat up the stores of food in each district.

Wenworth was a castle of average size and strength, though beginning to be thought a trifle old-fashioned and less comfortable than some of the newer castles. It consisted of a massive stone tower or *donjon*, standing in a walled courtyard which contained some lean-to sheds with thatched roofs. Attached to this inner courtyard was a much bigger one, the *outer bailey*, surrounded by a *curtain* wall which the Earl had recently strengthened with some round towers. A moat, fed by a small stream, encircled the entire castle.

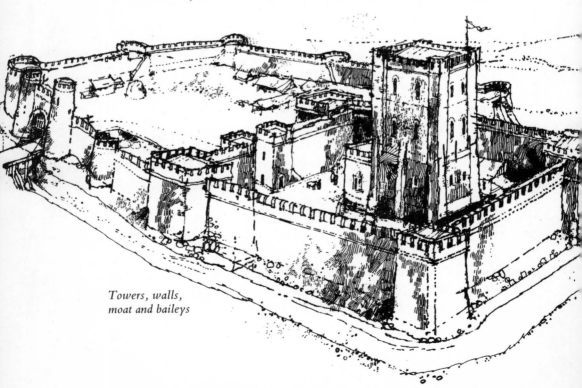

Towers, walls, moat and baileys

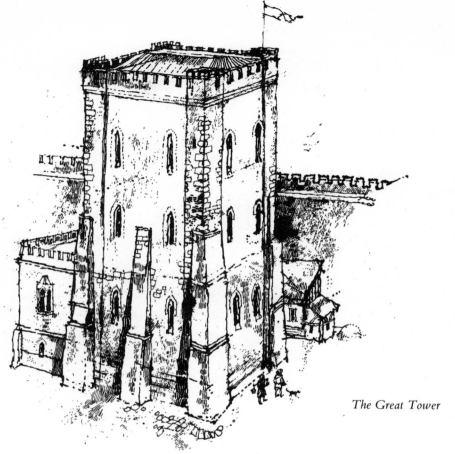

The Great Tower

The great tower, seventy feet high with walls eight feet thick, was the strongest point of defence. Its plan was very simple, for there were only two floors above a basement-storeroom. At the top there were battlements, with a wall-walk for the soldiers who could see across country for miles. There was no entrance at ground level.

If you were a visitor—or an enemy—you could only get into the tower by going up a flight of steps to the door. These steps were in the *forebuilding* which also contained the chapel above and a prison cell below. At the top of the steps, you passed through the porter's lodge into the Great Hall, the largest and most important room in the castle.

The Great Hall

When you came in from the open air, the Hall seemed bare
and gloomy, for it was lit by only two windows set in deep
recesses. There was no chimney-place but a hearth in the
middle of the floor and the smoke had to find its way out of
the door and windows. That was why the walls were
freshly whitewashed every spring after the winter's grime
had been cleaned away.

There was very little furniture. Two high-backed chairs
stood on a low platform against one wall; there were several
wooden benches and an iron-hinged *livery cupboard* for salt
vessels, dishes, pickles and spices. Tables were stacked to one
side because each table-top could be lifted off its *trestles* which
were shaped like a carpenter's sawing-bench.

The treasury

The Hall was the centre of life indoors. The lord met his tenants there, listened to their grievances, collected rents and punished wrong-doers in the *Barony Court*. The people of the household ate their meals and gathered there for merry-making and ceremonies. Most of the men slept there on benches, or wrapped in cloaks on the floor amid the rushes. The ordinary man owned nothing except his clothes and the knife at his belt. He looked to his lord for food and shelter but he did not expect privacy or comfort.

Cut in the thickness of the wall was a little room called the *Treasury*. It contained the lord's best wine and a chest filled with rolls of parchment on which were written agreements which the lord and his ancestors had made with various tenants. Another chest contained his treasure. There was a leather bag of gold coins and a collection of rings, jewelled brooches, silver cups, dishes and candlesticks.

The lord's bedchamber

The Hall and the solar

In one corner of the Hall stood the *well-head*, with its chain and bucket ready to bring up water from the well in the basement. A doorway led to the spiral staircase and another door opened into a passage at whose end was a *privy-chamber* or lavatory.

The *solar*, next to the Hall, was the lord's private room. Here were two windows with wide ledges for seats and a great hooded fireplace. The lower part of the walls was painted in a criss-cross pattern of green and gold and the countess had hung up a large tapestry which her sister had sent her from France.

Behind a partition, the lord's sleeping-chamber contained a great double-bed whose frame was laced with ropes to support a feather mattress and its linen sheets, quilt and fur coverlet. Coloured hangings surrounded the bed but these were pulled back during the day when the bed provided a comfortable seat. A couple of *truckle-beds*, low frames with a mattress, could be pulled out from under the bed and on them slept the lady's maid and perhaps a nurse or a teenage daughter.

The second floor of the *tower* contained a number of sleeping chambers for guests, knights and the household officials. There was also a large dormitory for the maid-servants and this served as the sewing-room by day.

The countess was careful to see that her maidens behaved modestly and did not spend too long in the Hall gossiping with the men.

A maid-servant

Steward and messengers

The people of the household

The head of the household was, of course, the baron himself, but he was often absent, since it was his duty to attend the king from time to time and also to fight in the royal army.

In his absence, his wife ruled the household. She, too, travelled a good deal, visiting her manors and a nunnery in which she took an interest.

After the lord and his lady, the most important person in the castle was the *steward*. He acted as general manager, watching over all its affairs and seeing that each official carried out his job. At Wenworth, the steward was Sir Walter Tracy, a knight holding land of his own and not much below the lord in rank. Some stewards travelled everywhere with the family but Sir Walter lived permanently at the castle because the lord owned several manors in the neighbourhood.

The word *wardrobe* meant a place for storing valuable goods, and the *wardrober* had charge of all the stores. He sat with the steward each evening examining the daily accounts, for every item was written down on the *household roll* like this:

> Delivered from the wardrobe to the kitchen,
> 12 lb sugar, 2 lb pepper, 6 lb almonds, 16 lb rice.
> For the chapel, for candles, 10 lb of wax.
> For the carriage of 2 tuns of wine from Southampton, 12 shillings. For the expenses of Simon going there, 2 shillings.

The wardrober's clerk wrote these accounts and the *chaplain* or priest helped with the letters which the lord's messengers carried to various parts of the kingdom. A messenger was envied by the other servants, for he received two pence a day wages, money for food and drink on his journeys and, when he carried good news, he often received a gift as well.

Writing the household roll

The almoner

It was a religious duty for a great lady to help the poor and, in her household, the countess had a priest called the *almoner* to see that *alms* were given every day to the poor, as well as food left over from the table.

The chaplain's clerk looked after the sacred vessels, candlesticks and robes used in the chapel. When a move took place, he would see that these were loaded on a pack-horse, with a portable altar so that Mass could be said on the journey.

Travelling arrangements were organised by the *marshal* who had fifty or sixty horses in his care. The most valuable of these were the knights' warhorses, but these were kept solely for battle and tournaments, and on journeys a knight rode a *palfrey*, a good horse for everyday use, while lesser folk were mounted on working nags called *rounseys*.

In addition, the marshal had charge of the carthorses and *sumpter horses*, strong pack-animals that carried heavy loads. Grooms attended the horses and the smith or *farrier* kept them shod. It was often a problem to find enough iron for horseshoes, wheel rims and fittings of the wagons. Manors near the castle sent in oats and grass for the horses but on journeys these had to be bought along the route.

When the household moved, its people, wagons and pack-train formed a long procession that wound slowly across country, covering about thirty kilometres a day. The marshal had to make careful arrangements to feed and lodge them all but the lord, his lady and their attendants would ride ahead to stay the night at an abbey or at the castle of a cousin.

The marshal

Food and drink

People rose early and, since they ate only a hunk of bread for breakfast, dinner was taken at ten or eleven o'clock in the morning. The preparations began at sunrise.

Under the wardrober's sharp eye, the food for the day was issued to the cook—so many eels and eggs, so many pounds of rice, so much beef. These stores, laid in for months ahead, were kept in the basement or in store sheds in the inner bailey.

Meanwhile, the baker had already started work. The amounts of flour and yeast were carefully noted, since bakers were well known for their dishonest tricks. The finest bread, called *wastel*, was a white loaf for the lord's table; whole-wheat bread was made for the rest of the household and there was also common-wheat bread, and darker loaves made from barley and rye. A small *cocket loaf* was very good to eat, while *simnel* bread was twice cooked like biscuits.

The bakery

The kitchen

Some castles had a kitchen inside the tower, but at Wenworth the cooking was still done in a big shed-like kitchen that stood against the bailey wall. This meant that the food had to be carried across the yard and up the stairs into the Hall. Some people think that it must have been half cold and greasy, but meat was nearly always boiled and servants could carry the big iron cauldrons right into the Hall. A joint of venison or a goose roasted on the spit did not lose much heat if the cook made haste up the stairs. In some castles, covered passage-ways were built from the kitchen to the tower.

As long as there was plenty to eat, nobody complained if the food was not piping hot.

A capon for the cook

Meat, fish and vegetables

Beef, mutton, veal and pork were the usual meats. Everyone loved venison but it was a luxury set aside for the lord's table. Vast numbers of chickens and geese were eaten, for they cost no more than a penny or two each. They were brought in alive from the country and kept in pens until the cook wanted them. Their feathers were put aside to be used for pillows and feather beds. The best chickens, called *capons*, were fattened in coops. Eggs were used in fantastic numbers, for we hear of 3000 being supplied for Easter week at three to four pence a hundred!

The cook needed great quantities of fish all the year round, because Fridays, and often Wednesdays and Saturdays too, were meatless days. The castle had its own fishpond and huge numbers of eels were supplied by the manors. People preferred sea fish when they could get it, especially fresh herrings, plaice and cod. They even liked whale meat and porpoises but everyone grew tired of salted herrings all through Lent.

Every district made its own butter and cheese and the wardrober kept stocks of hams, sides of bacon and barrels of salt fish and salt meat. He would buy great cheeses weighing 90 to 130 kilograms each in the town market.

No-one cared much for green vegetables which they called 'worts' but they had to eat plenty of dried beans and peas when meat was scarce in winter. Often, they had to make do with a bowl of thick vegetable soup called *pottage*. The villagers grew cabbages, onions, leeks and radishes but potatoes were unknown.

The castle had its own orchard with apple, pear, plum, medlar and cherry trees. Occasionally, a rare fruit called an orange appeared on the lord's table.

In the orchard

A salt-merchant

Spices and herbs

Salt was absolutely essential because salted meat and fish had to be eaten in winter when there was only enough hay to keep a few animals alive. Travelling salt-merchants brought their loaded packhorses to the castle or servants were sent to town to buy salt at three to four pence a bushel. Most of the salt came from the coast where seawater was evaporated in salt-pans.

Since meat was often salted and nearly rotten, people used all kinds of sauces to disguise its taste. Spices cost a lot of money and the wardrober kept a special *spice account*, separate from the household roll.

The commonest spices were *ginger* and *pepper*. Both came from the East and cost about ten pence a pound; *cloves* were even more expensive but *cinnamon* was cheaper and so was another hot spice called *galingale*. Other spices included *corriander*, *caraway seeds*, *cummin*, much used to flavour chicken, *nut-megs* and their dried rind called *mace*.

The castle herb-garden produced mustard, parsley, sage, garlic, fennel, hyssop and borage. The costliest herb, *saffron*, came from Spain where millions of crocuses were grown, since it was their stamens that produced the bright yellow saffron.

The lady of the household took a close interest in the herb garden because she had to see to the making of medicines and ointments. Herbs, honey, vinegar and wild plants like ivy and celandine were used in making remedies for aches, pains and wounds.

Using a pestle and mortar to grind spices and herbs

Sugar, wine and ale

As well as hot spicy dishes, people loved sweet ones. They kept bees but did not rely entirely on honey because sugar-cane was now widely grown in the Mediterranean lands. It reached England in the form of the *sugar-loaf*, a hard packed mass that had to be pounded in the kitchen.

To drink, there were two choices—wine, if you belonged to the upper class, ale, if you did not. Milk was drunk by very young children but mead had gone out of fashion and cider was not popular outside the west country.

A little wine was produced in England but most wines came from Gascony in France.

Pounding a sugar-loaf

The butler

The ale-wife

The castle's store of drink was kept in the *buttery* in charge of the *butler* who had to order sufficient wine each year but not too much because it did not keep well. He also had the tricky job of transporting the wine when the household moved and, for this, he hired special carts at a penny a mile for each big cask or *tun*.

The butler prepared wine in various ways. In addition to red and white wines, he served sweetened and spiced wines and others in which he mixed liquorice, cloves and fennel in order to cure people of colds and stomach-ache.

Ale, made from barley and also from wheat and oats, was drunk by everyone, including children. An *ale-wife* did the brewing with the aid of her women helpers; she made about 200 gallons at a time, and since the cost was only a halfpenny a gallon the castle servants had a generous allowance at dinner time. An allowance of ale was given to the serfs of the manor when they brought in the lord's harvest. Hops which are used nowadays to flavour beer were not yet used in brewing.

Earl Richard

Morning at Wenworth Castle

Let us spend a summer's day at Wenworth Castle in the year 1250.

At day-break, the household begins to stir, and in the lord's bedchamber the nurse rises from her pallet, puts on her gown and goes to attend to her ladyship's youngest child in her cradle. While she is feeding her, a maidservant brings a ewer of warm water from the kitchen for the baby's bath.

Meanwhile, the lady's maid who also sleeps in the same room, has washed and dressed herself and has pushed her truckle-bed under the big bed.

Behind its curtains, Earl Richard wakes and comes out in his undershirt to wash at a basin on a stand. He is very particular about cleanliness and will bath in a tub at the end of the week. He uses soap made from wood ash mixed in scented mutton fat. Instead of shaving, he rubs his chin with a piece of pumice stone.

He dresses in linen drawers, hose that stretch above the knee, a loose tunic pulled over his head and a fur-lined surcoat with wide sleeves. When he has put on his *coif* or cap, he goes into the solar where the steward is already waiting.

While they talk business, the countess dresses with the help of her maid. Her clothes are very similar to those of her husband—linen shift, knee-length stockings kept up by embroidered garters, tunic fastened by a brooch, over-tunic and a warm mantle, for the hour is early and the castle is always cold. Her maid braids her hair and hides it under a *wimple*, a linen band that goes under her chin and is covered by a white cap of stiffened linen.

Countess Margaret

At the castle

Accompanied by the chief members of the household, the earl and his lady go to Mass in the chapel where the service is taken by Abbot Hugh of Farley, a guest who is staying at the castle.

After mass, the lord and his steward deal with affairs of the manor. Will Bird wishes to pay a rent for his land instead of working three days a week on the lord's land but the steward is not keen on the idea of making him a freeman. Let him ask again in a year's time. John Shepherd's son has gone to the abbey to be a monk-in-training; his father shall pay four shillings. The reeve reports several cases of beasts straying into the hay meadow; the owners are to appear at the Manor Court with two men caught cutting down a tree in the forest. The Earl agrees to have the water-mill mended but the reeve must find men to clean out the castle moat. Now, there is the matter of buying the manor next to Povey . . .

*Mending
the water-mill*

The huntsmen

    While this everyday business is being settled, an air of excitement runs through the castle. Everyone knows that the lord is going hunting with the abbot, and the horses are ready in the yard with the grooms checking girths and harness, while the knights stand about waiting.

    At last, he appears with his guest, the abbot. A page holds his horse while he mounts and then he goes across to have a word with Robert the huntsman who stands with his whip in the midst of his pack of restless hounds.

The daily round

A horn sounds and the gaily dressed party canters across the drawbridge towards the forest, watched enviously by all who have to stay behind. Hunting is a passion. The poorest peasant loves to snare rabbits and many nobles care for little else in life but the chase. The king has granted Earl Richard the precious right of *vert and venison* which means that he may hunt the deer and wild boar on his own land.

As the hunting party disappears from view, the people of the castle return to their tasks. In the kitchen yard, the cook bawls orders; a servant comes in, bent under a load of fire-wood; another carries a side of beef; water is fetched from the well, spices from the wardrobe, fish, flour and eggs from the store. A little maid goes down to the herb garden, while another girl begins the tedious job of pounding sugar. Presently, they will start plucking chickens, pigeons and various small birds.

Servants

Armourer and his boy

In the armoury, the armourer checks his stocks of lances, bows, swords and mail. The paid soldiers possess their own weapons but replacements may be needed and the armourer knows that when the local men come to do castle-guard, they usually come poorly equipped. So he keeps a good stock of weapons, bowstrings and arrows, especially the short heavy bolts for the crossbows.

One of his problems is to keep chain mail in good order because its metal scales soon become rusty. This morning, he puts several suits in a barrel, sprinkles them with sand and vinegar, turns the barrel on its side and tells his boy to roll it up and down. When the mail is taken out, all the rust has disappeared. Shields and helmets are polished with bran and put back in their racks.

Castle repairs

Everyday tasks

Down at the gatehouse, two soldiers are engaged in greasing the winding gear of the portcullis, the hinges of the great double doors and the runners of the drawbridge. In peaceful times, the drawbridge is left in position for people and carts to cross the moat but the doors are shut and the portcullis lowered every day at sunset.

The carpenter and a thatcher are repairing the roof of the buttery and the carpenter grumbles about the unending work on these wooden buildings. He says it is time the earl rebuilt them all in stone.

As he works, the carpenter can hear the tap-tap of the mason's hammer, for his friend is up on the battlements replacing some stonework. After that, he will inspect the lead roof and gutters of the tower because damp is the biggest enemy to the timbers and fittings of the castle.

Meanwhile, Sir Walter the steward is seated in the Hall where he questions the reeve or village foreman who gives him an exact account of all the animals and their young on the manor. A clerk writes this down and the reeve is told to supply six piglets and six fat lambs on the morrow. He must see that the villagers start to cut the lord's hay next week.

The Countess Margaret has a dozen things to see to. First, she speaks to the nurse about the baby's health, but she does not stay for more than a few minutes. Bringing up children is not the business of a great lady. The nurse will feed and wash the child, teach her to talk, dose her with medicine and take complete charge of her early years. Her mother expects her to grow into an obedient well-mannered girl and, when she is about fifteen, her parents will arrange her marriage to a nobleman.

A lesson in archery

Manners and clothes

Lady Margaret's sons are already away from home, one
in the household of the Earl of Leicester, the other with the
Bishop of Winchester. There they will 'learn manners', how
to behave at table and towards grown-ups, how to ride,
fight and to read a letter or a document. At present, two
young nobles are staying at Wenworth and the countess
looks into the Hall to make sure they are at their lessons with
the chaplain.

Penmanship

The tailor

Next, she goes upstairs to the big chamber where her damsels and the sewing-women are at work. All members of the household are given clothes as part of their wages. The nurse and her ladyship's clerk receive costlier robes than, say, the cook and the butler who have two pence a day in wages and clothes worth nine shillings every year.

New clothes are given at Christmas but the work of making them goes on all through the year. Lady Margaret decides the cloth for each garment and the proper amount of decoration and trimming.

She sends her tailor to London twice a year to buy cloth. Most cloths are woollens, such as *burnet*, a strong material for hard wear, *perse*, a much better cloth, *Lincoln scarlet* and *kersey*, a ribbed cloth much used for making hose. Coarse *russets* and *chalons* are bought for the lower servants but silk cloth, some of it brocaded with silver threads, comes from Italy and is very expensive. So are *damask*, a heavy material from Damascus, and *sandal*, a beautiful foreign cloth as light as silk. These are bought for her ladyship's own gowns.

The countess and her tailor

The lady of the household

The tailor will also buy a large quantity of linen for making sheets, pillow-slips, table-cloths, napkins and towels, as well as finer linens for wimples and underwear.

The countess discusses these purchases, telling the tailor to buy about eighty ells of cloth (an ell is 1·15 metres) but not to lay out more than four pounds altogether. He should pay from two to nine pence an ell for linen and from one to eight shillings an ell for woollens. She would also like him to look out for some squirrel fur to re-line her lord's winter gown.

After she has written a number of letters and has made arrangements for a supply of candles for the chapel, the countess and her maid take a walk in the open air with her little pet dog.

They go down into the outer bailey to stroll in the sun-shine to the walled garden which the Earl had made for her. She loves its lilies, marigolds, roses and gillyflowers, its neat gravelled paths, mulberry trees and climbing vines. She has a row of beehives but the mason has not finished the great new dovecot which he has promised to build.

The washerwomen are laying out sheets to dry, the miller's cart laden with sacks of flour comes in over the drawbridge and two sturdy milkmaids, on their way back from the meadow outside the walls, rest their pails for a moment and curtsey to the ladies as they pass.

In the castle garden

Return from the hunt

Dinner at the castle

As dinner time draws near, tables are put up in the Hall and are spread with clean linen. Servants set the top table with salts, drinking cups and spoons made of silver. On the lower tables, earthenware cups and wooden or horn spoons are set for the lower ranks but the household officials have *mazers*, wooden cups with silver rims, to drink from.

Each place is set with a thick slice of day-old bread called a *trencher*. This serves as a plate and, after dinner, the gravy-soaked trenchers will be thrown to the dogs or gathered up and sent to the poor.

The shrill note of a horn announces the return of the hunters and the servants run to see how they have fared. Two men can be seen coming through the main gate carrying a fine buck slung on a pole. Someone calls out that they have killed two others and everyone grins with pleasure because, later in the week, when the venison is roasted, there may be some morsels for the lower tables!

The ceremony of handwashing

Dinner commences with the ceremony of hand-washing. When the earl, his lady and their guests have taken their places, pages bring bowls of water to each person who dips his fingers and wipes them on a towel laid across the page's arm. The two little boys from noble families carry out this duty.

Meanwhile, the rest of the household wash their hands at wash-stands as they enter the Hall. Then they sit down in order of rank, the humblest folk farthest away from the top table.

The Hall marshal

Table manners: two courses

The first course is announced by trumpet and the *hall marshal* brings in the principal dish on a silver platter, followed by servants bearing lesser dishes. These are set down, one dish between two persons; it is good manners to serve your neighbour first and to pick out the nicest morsels for a guest. He takes his own knife out of its sheath and, although he has no fork, he uses his fingers politely, not licking them but wiping them on his bread.

Table manners are very important and these are some of the rules of polite behaviour which children learn from their nurse:

> Don't bite your bread but break it; don't talk with your mouth full; don't wipe your knife on the table-cloth; eat quietly and don't blow on your food if it is hot; wipe your mouth on your napkin before drinking; don't let your dog be a nuisance at table.

Here are the dishes served at the top table:

First course   Boiled mutton served with a pudding and spiced sauce

Brawn (meat of a pig's head) with a sharp sauce

A pike stuffed with almonds

Capon of great fatness

Pheasants

A baked custard in pastry

Second course Venison cooked in a stew of spiced corn

Sucking pig stuffed with forcemeat

Rabbit—the white meat only

Eels cooked in a pie

Chicken in saffron with egg yolks

Fried brawn with vinegar sauce

A fruit pie

Dinner-time

Dinner

Third course A white curd and meat cooked in almonds
Quince pie
Curlews, pigeons, snipe
A great perch, baked
Eggs in jelly
Rabbit cooked whole
Marzipan sweetmeats, fritters
'Little lost eggs'—eggs and mincemeat in pastry

At the lower tables, the food is not so rich. Bowls of thick meat soup are followed by boiled beef, eel pie and dishes of chopped chicken and pork in a hot ginger sauce.

The butler makes sure that everyone at the top table is served with wine. The lord passes his own silver cup to his lady and then to his guest. This is an ancient custom in which the cup is held by one hand under the bowl.

Passing the cup

The lower table

The lord sometimes sends the remains of a tasty dish down to the lower tables and today he tells his page to take a piece of venison to Robert the huntsman. Robert, a well-known joker, dares to send back a lump of fat pork and this is received with loud laughter.

The ale jug is passed round and someone calls for a song, so Ralph the carter is made to stand up and sing one of his songs, half made up as he goes along, about the marvellous adventures of the miller's boy who rode his old horse to London town.

After dinner has ended with a second washing of hands the people go back to their work. It is June, when the days are longest and everyone will be out of doors until the sun has disappeared.

Work and play

Supper is taken in the evening, a lighter meal with egg dishes and cheese. Then, while the steward and the wardrober pore over their accounts, some of the others play chess or draughts while the ladies in the solar take up their embroidery.

No-one wastes candles in summertime, and when the light has faded everyone goes to bed—everyone, that is, except the watchman up on the tower and the guards in the gatehouse.

On the morrow, the round of work and play begins again. The earl has decided to go hawking to try out a new falcon, a splendid bird which he keeps on a perch in the solar. The falconer has trained it to kill a heron and return to its master's wrist.

Before they go hawking, there is to be arms-practice for the knights and soldiers, lessons in the use of weapons for the pages and shooting at the butts for the archers.

The falconer

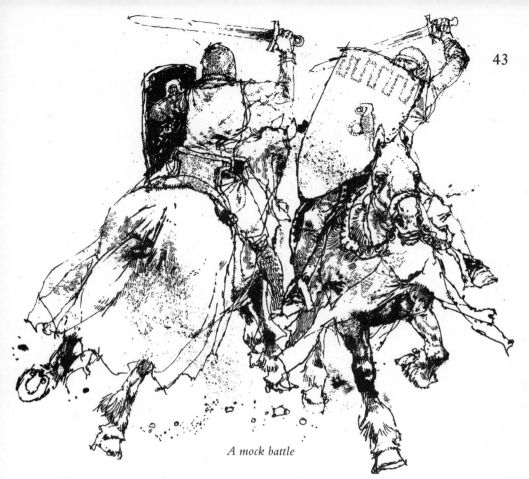

A mock battle

Tournaments are not a series of single combats but are still mock battles in which groups of knights fight with light-weight swords. Boys have to learn to charge at speed with shield and lance; war-horses need regular schooling and the archers have to practise rapid fire with both types of bow. They use the short bow with which the Welsh are the great experts and the more complicated cross-bow which is cumbersome but more powerful and absolutely essential for defence of the castle.

All this training is a necessary part of life for the ruling class and the Earl always remembers that while Wenworth Castle is his home, it is also a fortress.

Book list

Castles, R. J. Unstead (A. & C. Black)
The Medieval Castle, M. E. Reeves (Longman)
Castles, B. H. St J. O'Neil (H.M.S.O.)
Scottish Castles, W. Douglas Simpson (H.M.S.O.)
Castles in Britain, W. Douglas Simpson (Batsford)
Castles, R. Allen Brown (Batsford)
Exploring Castles, W. Douglas Simpson (Routledge)
Castles and Fortresses, R. R. Sellman (Methuen)